APP is for APPLIQUÉ

DIANNE S. HIRE

American Quilter's Society

P.O. Box 3290 • Paducah, KY 42002-3290
Fax 270-898-1173 • e-mail: orders@AQSquilt.com

Located in Paducah, Kentucky, the American Quilter's Society (AQS) is dedicated to promoting the accomplishments of today's quilters. Through its publications and events, AQS strives to honor today's quiltmakers and their work and to inspire future creativity and innovation in quiltmaking.

EXECUTIVE BOOK EDITOR: ELAINE BRELSFORD
BOOK EDITOR: LINDA BAXTER LASCO
COPY EDITOR: CHRYSTAL ABHALTER
PROOFREADER: JOANN TREECE
GRAPHIC DESIGN: ELAINE WILSON
COVER DESIGN: MICHAEL BUCKINGHAM
QUILT PHOTOGRAPHY: CHARLES R. LYNCH
HOW-TO PHOTOGRAPHY: CHARLES R. LYNCH, UNLESS OTHERWISE NOTED

ATTENTION PHOTOCOPYING SERVICE: Please note the following—Publisher and author give permission to print pages 88–94 for personal use only.

Additional copies of this book may be ordered from the American Quilter's Society, PO Box 3290, Paducah, KY 42002-3290, or on-line at www.AmericanQuilter.com.

Text © 2013, Author, Dianne S. Hire
Artwork © 2013, American Quilter's Society

American Quilter's Society
P.O. Box 3290 • Paducah, KY 42002-3290
Fax 270-898-1173 • e-mail: orders@AQSquilt.com

Library of Congress Control Number: 2013952753

COVER: CLAMSHELL IN SILK. See project pages 10–13.

TITLE PAGE: CIRQUE DU QUILT, detail. Full quilt on page 71.

DEDICATION

To my one and only, my partner in design and in life.

It is to Terry that this book belongs.

Your encouragement and love have allowed the sparkle to continue.

Without you, such designs would have been only mind's-eye inklings.

Once upon a time you said, "Never look back."

And that's how we've lived, longing for Design Perfection in our eternal home.

LEFT: EBULLIENCE, detail. Full quilt on page 32.

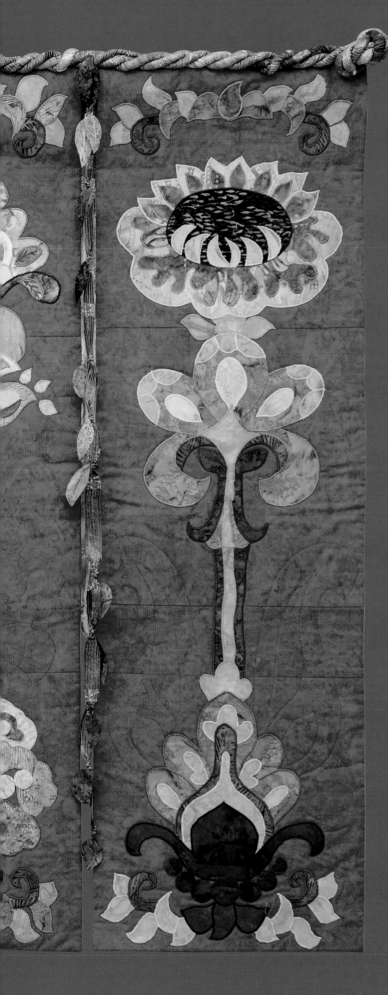

CONTENTS

LEFT: HIGH ANXIETY. Full quilt on page 52.

INTRODUCTION

L et's admit it. Within most of us, several quilt personalities exist. We all own a design vocabulary, of sorts. There's the quirky calico-me who adores tiny motifs, 1930s prints, and classic richly sueded browns. On the other hand, the complete opposite is true. I'm continually inspired by the vibrant color and pattern found all around.

Since it isn't a dominant feature in my pieces, the unexpected quilt personality that most folks never see is that I'm enamored with appliqué and its elaborate intricacies.

BELOW: Array of perfectly arranged, fabulous fringed scarves
PHOTO: Dianne S. Hire

Once upon a time in the distant past of my retailing days, I recall long meetings where, to keep my mind from totally wandering, I doodled flowing, flowery, scroll-type things as a boredom reliever. But *whoa*, sometimes the sketches would catch my interest. I wish I'd saved them. How fun it would be to see them now—to view whether or not they relate to that with which we are about to engage?

Saved in a box or thrown into a designated basket, there are many such "Di-doodles" of which portions are incorporated into this book.

In a mode I call "fast-lane design," the brainstorm came in about three days. Find a dozen or so specialists who love appliqué and are willing to take 14 line-drawn Di-doodle designs and construct different appliqué blocks into a quilt. The app-experts faced only one caveat—*interpret in any way you wish and in any and every way possible.* They were invited to create quilts using their own fave fabrics, fave methods, and fave colors. Such diverse techniques are a part of the book's strength, methinks, and such awaits you with your own interpretations.

I spent hours fast and furiously Di-doodling small sketches for an overall idea. Later, when satisfied with the small sketch, I sketched a full-scale 12½" x 12½" block drawing on graph paper. Always, these were approved by Sir Hilary in his supervisory capacity while trying to snitch the pen.

Sir Hilary preparing for a long nap on selected fabrics
PHOTO: Terry Hire

TOP RIGHT: Often I dismantle necklaces to fill the bead bottles. These, displayed at an open market in Marrakesh, are too beautiful to tear apart.
PHOTO: Dianne S. Hire

BOTTOM RIGHT: Beads on author's shelves are colorized, ready to use. **PHOTO:** Terry Hire

Wonderful stacked bracelets at a vendor's booth in Morocco **PHOTO:** Dianne S. Hire

There are 14 different blocks with one motif that serves as a unifying theme—a horizontal array of leaves at the bottom of each vase/urn/holder. With such diversity in the central design of each block, something cohesive must be drawn to hold the blocks together. My intention was that a finished quilt with multiple blocks would maintain design integrity through the use of this motif repetition.

Few instructions were given to the app-experts. Each was a skilled specialist with a toolbox of proficiency and high quality talent who needed little from me. "Here are my line drawings but use *your method, your color sense, your interpretation, your approach to structure, and your style.*"

Over the next 12 months, each app-expert opted not to share during the creative process. The left hand did not want to be influenced by what the right hand was doing—whether by color, block arrangement, or technique. Half the fun for them was keeping secrets.

At last the quilts were ready for presentation at (what else?) a quilter's champagne potluck celebration with food, quilts, laughter, camaraderie, and chocolate, of course. The day we got to see the finished quilts, we all were astounded by what was in front of us. Gasps were heard around the room. The moment was electric; it was magical. All at once, we were seeing a remarkable mixture of styles—intricate with simple, elaborate with effortless, complex with straightforward. Not only were the quiltmakers proficient in the technique, they were a little bit witty and certainly creative.

They confirmed that the possibilities are endless when a concept is embraced and liberated into reality. These are truly the best app-experts in the world, right here and in a book I'm authoring. I'm so very honored.

Take a little time to compare how each person created the blocks, how each added personal touches in fabric and colors as well as how each interpreted the designs. In every case, you will see a brilliant collection of wonderfully colorful and distinctively appliquéd quilts. Many opted for embellishments of threads, beads, and buttons. Well, why not, if the blocks are asking you to put them there?

So, let's see what awaits you. I hope you like the designs as much as I. I cannot wait to see your own adaptations of my Di-doodles.

> **Note:** Instructions for joining the blocks into full-size quilts are not included. They are meant to show the variety of possibilities and to inspire your own unique use of these designs.

BELOW: Group of beautiful app-experts at the champagne potluck. Shared joy for having actually finished on time! FRONT ROW (LEFT TO RIGHT): Glenna, Sally, Gail, Susan, Pat. MIDDLE ROW (LEFT TO RIGHT): Janet, Steve, Author, Rocky, Alice. BACK ROW (LEFT TO RIGHT): Sue, Ruth. Missing were: Arlaine, Teresa, and Sabra.
PHOTO: Terry Hire

14 BLOCKS & 15 QUILTS

CLAMSHELL IN SILK

CLAMSHELL IN SILK, 18¾" x 18¾", made by the author

The Focus Block

After all of the blocks had been selected, I, too, felt the need to complete one of the blocks and chose Clamshell.

But why silk? The real question I always ask… "Why not?" I'd never done anything like this, and if it turned out to be a complete failure, deleting it from the manuscript was only one finger away and the trash can is nearby to receive the flunked block. However, I love this one-block mini quilt. Its exquisite silk colorations capture my heart.

I wanted to hand appliqué these sumptuous dupioni silks (Fig. 1) and surprisingly, it turned out to be a very easy choice.

Fig. 1. Who can resist such an array of lushly vibrant and colorful dupioni silks? I don't even want to try. **PHOTO:** Dianne S. Hire

Sewing Instructions

1. Using a light box, lightly trace the design with a pencil onto the front of the background fabric (Fig. 2). The pale yellow silk was a good choice; darker fabric would be more difficult to see through and would require a white pencil for copying.

2. Gather your supplies (Fig. 3).

3. Turn the original paper design so that it faces the light box; copy each individual component onto freezer paper (Fig. 4, page 12).

4. From the freezer paper, cut out each individual unit on the traced line with sharp paper scissors.

5. Iron the freezer paper designs onto the back of the selected fabrics. Cut around the designs, leaving at least ¼" of silk fabric beyond the freezer paper. Finger press the fabric edges under and press with an iron (Fig. 5, page 12). If there are any unruly threads, spritz enough spray starch into a little bowl such as the plastic top of a spray starch can (Fig. 4, page 12) and apply onto the back with your fingers and iron again.

Fig. 2. With a pencil, lightly draw your design onto front side of background fabric. **PHOTO:** Dianne S. Hire

Fig. 3. An array of silks lying on the drawn soft yellow background. How can this not be beautiful? Will I be able to execute the design without messing up the fabrics? Let's see. **PHOTO:** Dianne S. Hire

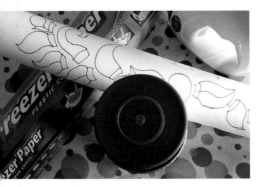

Fig. 4. Rolled up freezer paper with individually drawn components of Clamshell. *Note:* use green top as a handy holder for sprayed liquid starch. **PHOTO:** Dianne S. Hire

Fig. 5. See the ¼" green edges overlapped on the back of the freezer paper design. When using silk, trim the ¼" down a bit just before appliquéing the design to the background. **PHOTO:** Dianne S. Hire

Fig. 6. Fabric auditions—some will not be used for the finished block. **PHOTO:** Dianne S. Hire

6. Fabric auditions are being held (Fig. 6); some designs are ready to be appliquéd. It will be interesting to see which of these make the cut and which are pitched into the scrap bag.

7. Just like a puzzle, find which designs must overlap others; appliqué the underlying ones first. This leaf has two fabrics; stitch the parts together before placing onto the yellow background (Fig. 7, page 13).

8. See how the jigsaw puzzle begins to take shape. For me, it seemed easiest to begin at the leaf base and work up the design. You begin wherever it works for you. I keep the freezer paper in place until ready to apply the designs to the background (Fig. 8, page 13).

9. Using two colors for the foliage—blue with green instead of two greens—makes for a more interesting visual (Fig. 9, page 13).

10. You can see the design was changed a bit (Fig. 10, page 13). Instead of creating individual scallops, I opted to make them all the same and use one soft blue continuous fabric underneath. With these designs, you are given permission to make such executive decisions.

Tips for Crisp Points

❋ Keep the freezer paper on the leaf to accomplish a really nice point on your leaf.

❋ Align the two points—the fabric leaf point and the drawn one where the leaf will be placed.

❋ Sew the point, then sew approximately ½" down on each side of the point.

❋ Gently remove freezer paper and complete appliquéing the leaf in place. Now, you see that there is a point to all of this!

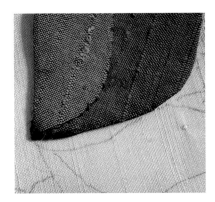

Fig. 7. Two shades of green silk are sewn together before the single leaf is appliquéd in place. PHOTO: Dianne S. Hire

Fig. 8. Units in place, ready to be appliquéd. See Tips for Crisp Points on page 12. PHOTO: Dianne S. Hire

Fig. 9. Half of foliage is appliquéd. PHOTO: Dianne S. Hire

11. Many layers placed upon each other make a fun brainteaser to figure out which is first to be sewn. Complete all overlaps of fabrics until the appliqué is finished (Fig. 11).

12. The block. Finished. I think there will be more changes. A photograph shows imperfections in color choices as well as that strangely shaped red scallop, bottom left (Fig. 12a).

Note the changes between what I thought was the finished block and its final incarnation (Fig. 12b). I added hot pink dots, lots of embroidery threads, and texture with long-stitch hand quilting in the pale yellow background.

Fig. 10. Note the pale blue background onto which four shades of green scallops were applied. Who says the design must be finished exactly as presented? PHOTO: Dianne S. Hire

Fig. 11. The yummiest shades of my fave colors of periwinkle set off the yellow recurved point beyond the green scallops. PHOTO: Dianne S. Hire

Fig. 12a. The finished block; so I thought. It sat for a while and yes, it was changed before the final piece. PHOTO: Dianne S. Hire

Fig. 12b. The *real* finished block. PHOTO: Charles R. Lynch

Clamshell

Clamshell, 12" x 12", made by Teresa M. Fusco

The Focus Block

Teresa M. Fusco is a quiltmaker whose love of bold prints and lively color is evident in her Clamshell block. When first presented with the line drawn design, she created a single clamshell as a mini-quilt.

Exciting, glitzy fuchsia free-motion quilting with Sulky® Sliver™ not only gives sparkle as you view the quilt but also adds dimension to all the components. Note the critical places that Teresa's eye knew precisely where to drop in several different black-and-white prints, creating joyful eye candy.

Envisioning a colorful vase of clamshells, each one of a kind, she searched for fabric that glowed and watched the vase holding the shells come to life.

"When I was told to use my creativity and color palette, it turned me on. Just knowing I could create my own Teresa Clamshell made this so much fun; all I was given was a black-and-white drawing with a huge license to be artistically inventive!" And, this is exactly how you are to interpret the designs—open to your own personal preferences with permission granted to be artistically inventive.

Teresa treats us by sharing her favorite technique for appliqué, fondly calling it: *Raw-Edge Appliqué, Teresa's Way.*

1. Turn your pattern wrong-side up and tape it to a light box. If it is a simple design, a sunlit window works, too.

2. Redraw the pattern on regular paper; use a black marker to number each unit (Fig. 1). Why? There are 91 units in the Clamshell design! If you fail to number the pieces, it is highly likely you will mix them up.

3. Keeping the design wrong-side up, trace the entire pattern onto freezer paper, including the numbers. Cut all these pieces out and place in groups by rows corresponding to their placement in the design. This will certainly make it easier (Fig. 2).

Fig. 1. Number each of the 91 pieces to keep them in the correct location. **PHOTO:** Teresa M. Fusco

Fig. 2. All of these dazzling little pieces ironed onto freezer paper are the beginning of a stunning Clamshell. Note the rows already aligned, awaiting to be reset onto the background fabric. **PHOTO:** Teresa M. Fusco

Fig. 3. Now you see why you copy the pattern in black marker: it is easy to see through, even if dark fabric is used. PHOTO: Teresa M. Fusco

Fig. 4. The clamshells are coming to life as fabrics are placed into the vase. PHOTO: Teresa M. Fusco

4. Audition fabrics. Dig into your scrap bag for some eye-catching pieces.

5. Iron each freezer-paper template to the wrong-side of your chosen fabrics (Fig. 2, page 15). With a very sharp pair of paper scissors, cut each piece out along the edge of the paper and place in rows.

6. Select a background fabric. For a 12" block design, give yourself wiggle room and start with a 14" x 14" square. Iron into quarters, then on a diagonal to find the center of the background fabric. Tape it onto a light box (Fig. 3).

7. Start at the bottom (the leaves). Remove the ironed-on freezer paper from the fabric, place onto the background where it belongs on the see-through pattern (Fig. 4). Leave all edges loose in order to slip other units underneath. Tack the pieces with 1 to 2 dots of Roxanne® Glue-Baste-It to hold in place until you appliqué. Caution—do not over glue.

8. When all units are in place, gently press (not iron) the entire square.

9. Safety pin the block onto a piece of flat, no-loft cotton batting.

10. Prepare your sewing machine. Insert a topstitch needle and use your favorite Sulky Sliver™ or hologram thread. If you use a drop of silicone on the spool, often this will prevent any breakage. Drop the feed dogs and attach a free-motion machine quilting foot.

Your creative juices will be flowing as you free-motion raw-edge appliqué in contrasting Sulky Sliver, metallic, and/or rayon threads. A long stitch catches the light better than a short stitch, which imbeds into the surface and does not show off the beauty of the threads.

11. When the block is finished, you are ready to layer with your backing fabric and quilt as desired.

Teresa's Quilt

Nine blocks were first selected for a full-size quilt, but at a do-over session, Teresa added four more, splitting them in half to create an incredibly dynamic three-dimensional effect. Each block was shaped as an individual clamshell and, for emphasis, outlined with chartreuse edging. Fun quilting was done over several different purple backgrounds and onto the blocks with fuchsia, orange, and gold. Sliver and red rayon thread by Sulky cause the quilt to glow with light. The raw-edge appliquéd border exemplifies Teresa's colorful passion for life and for fabrics.

Meet Teresa M. Fusco

Teresa M. Fusco, born and raised in Long Island, New York, now resides in Valley Stream, New York. She is an artist, award-winning quilter, lecturer, and teacher.

Her dynamic personality is contagious as she brings enthusiasm for art to all of her classes. Teresa's work is collected by corporations and by private collectors.

PHOTO: John B. McSherry

CLAMSHELL, 52½" x 74", made by Teresa M. Fusco

Feathers II

Feathers II, 12" x 12", made by Glenna Graves Quigley

Fig. 1. A stack of potential fabrics; some may not work.
PHOTO: Glenna Graves Quigley

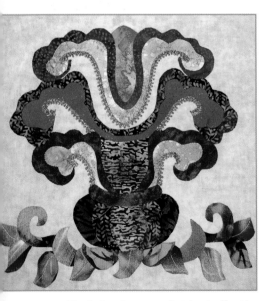

Fig. 2. Good use of color to accomplish diminishing light.
PHOTO: Glenna Graves Quigley

The Focus Block

App-expert Glenna Graves Quigley gratefully attributes Jeana Kimball teaching her special method of back-basting needle-turn hand appliqué (see page 80).

At the beginning of a project, it is important for Glenna to make a colorway decision for her complete quilt, as you see in the stack (Fig. 1). Preparation includes fabric choices. She allows the batiks to speak to her and conversation erupts between Glenna and her fabrics as she finds herself talking back.

Do you do this? Talking, that is? I do and often. I find that talking clarifies issues. How can you determine colors, scales, and combinations without having complete permission from your fabrics? How can you quilt without speaking to the sewing machine, complimenting good behavior and saying, no, no, no, to bad? It's usually noisy in my studio, voices are only mine, but ya gotta do this to clarify. (I tried to convince my iPad into completing the manuscript for this book, but that annoying device has a mind of its own and writes whatever it wants.)

Here is an image at the beginning of the Feathers II block assembly. Glenna plays with different shades of fabric to accomplish perspective around the base. At the center of the blue vase there is the appearance of light; depth is achieved with darker fabrics used as the vase curves toward the back (Fig. 2).

Glenna's Feathers II block was finished off using gold trim edging around the feathers (Fig. 3).

Fig. 3. Feathers are finished off with gold trim edging.
PHOTO: Glenna Graves Quigley

Glenna's Quilt

A s that first block came together, she noted that she was falling in love with the adventure. After only a month into the project, Glenna found herself already working on the third block. Note that in her completed quilt, FLOWER BASKETS (page 22), the gold was removed. Instead, there are small golden beads, almost as water droplets, on the feathers (Fig. 4).

Fig. 4. Feathers with gold trim removed, but replaced with water droplet golden beads.

Not making anything easy for herself, Glenna used metallic threads to hand embroider the blocks; for hand appliqué, she used Superior Machine Embroidery and YLI Silk for Appliqué. The twelve blocks surround a central thirteenth block, Lindy Loop, which was enlarged for the center medallion.

Notice those lovely little floaters in the sashing. Glenna improvised this design from an antique tin quilting template, translating a stitchery design into a superb fabric design. Since the antique template is in the public domain, you may also sketch this graceful little open tulip for your own use.

Meet Glenna Graves Quigley

Glenna Graves Quigley has been doing needlework since the age of seven and has earned multiple awards throughout the northeast for her exquisitely executed appliqué.

For 25 years she owned and operated a ceramics studio but found herself quilting while overseeing students painting on their ceramics. So it is that quilting took over. "Peanut," nickname for Clarence, a 16-pound cat, shares his home with Glenna and husband, Don, in Frankfort, Maine.

PHOTO: Donald Quigley

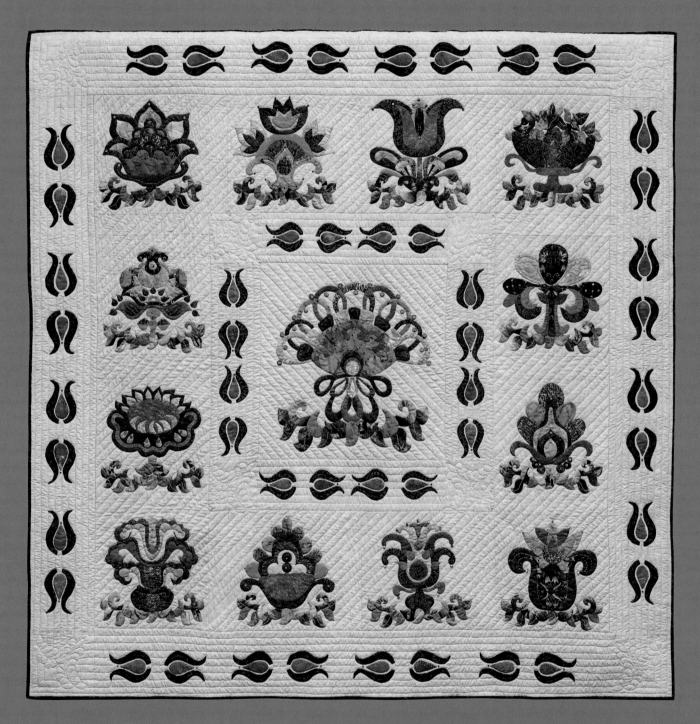

FLOWER BASKETS, *67" x 66",* made by Glenna Graves Quigley

FANTASY FLOWERS IN THE FOREST, 60½" x 75", made by Arlaine Furcht

Harp

Harp, 12" x 12", made by Alice Hobbs Parsons

The Focus Block

Let's go ahead and say it. Alice Hobbs Parsons creates some of the best quilts *ever*. Ordinarily, she leans toward a simple design style in an eclectic blending of gentle muted olive and neutral shades but always adds scrumptious color surprises to her mix. Look at her first fabric choices of the red/pinks layered upon olive/greens. Note how she added the surprising hushed plaid with a striking big dot (Fig. 1).

When presented with the intricacy of Harp, she noted that her standard operating procedure is "I have an option to change everything before I'm through."

That is why Alice discarded the first block created on a vertical swirly background (Fig. 2).

If you don't know it, Mainers are not known to waste anything. "Parsimonious" won't come near to explaining. It applies even to transplanted Kentuckians like Alice. Since she knew how much I believed her original Harp to be an incredible block, enhanced as it was with tiny embroidery stitches and petite colonial knots, she gifted me with lovely fabric note cards made from the discarded block (Figs. 3a–c). They may be framed and hung in my studio.

The challenge of designing and trusting her intuition is how Alice loves to work. By doing exactly that, she started over, combining her fave olive with other neutrals. Nothing should be a

Fig. 1. Alice's fabric stash selections
PHOTO: Alice Hobbs Parsons

Fig. 2. Beautiful but discarded Harp block on a background that Alice avowed made her eyes cross.
PHOTO: Alice Hobbs Parsons

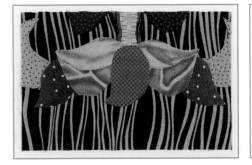

Figs. 3a–c. Three note cards whacked from Alice's discarded Harp block. "Mine!" said I, the pleased author.

Fig. 4. Fabrics in more muted colors were chosen as Alice went in the opposite direction from the first colorful block.
PHOTO: Alice Hobbs Parsons

Fig. 5. Compared to the original Harp block, this one is very subtle and Alice loves it!
PHOTO: Alice Hobbs Parsons

surprise, knowing Alice's bent toward textural art, but there it is—at the back of her photograph, let your eyes focus on the authentic pillowcase ticking—selected but not used (Fig. 4).

The entire block was fused this time because it was possible to lay out the individual pieces, prepared for fusing and cut to size, and make any necessary changes BEFORE fusing to the background. This block is rather subtle in comparison to her first one (Fig. 5).

Alice's Quilt

Alice used freezer paper, a light table, and a paper-backed fusible. The raw edges were machine straight stitched. Before the blocks were joined, each was embellished with a variety of embroidery stitches done with perle cotton.

Instead of piecing stripey things and/or appliquéing itsy-bitsy circles or even creating two-part leaves, Alice admits to using what she calls "cheaters." You go girl! That's exactly the beauty of these designs—to take them, alter them, and to make them yours.

I applaud her use of substitutions using printed commercial fabrics (Figs 6a–c). For example, in the Harp block, stripes were used instead of strip piecing, and printed leaves were utilized.

Fig. 6a. In Marbles, plaid fabric replaced pieced squares.

Fig. 6b. In Sunflower, printed circles substituted for cut ones.

Fig. 6c. In Low Vase yellow/turquoise leaf petals were used instead of ovals

A monotone of ecru perle cotton was used to "hand-embroider quilt" (embroidering through all three layers) and serve as embellishment as well. Alice hand quilted the background with the her free-style big stitch. Both of these techniques give EBULLIENCE a classic work-of-the-hand look, so dominant in her art and quilts (Figs. 7–8).

For Alice, EBULLIENCE offered challenges, decisions, changes, discoveries, excitement, frustration, patience, surprises, awe, beauty, completion, relief, and satisfaction. The word itself must be defined: "The quality of expressing feelings or ideas in an enthusiastic manner."

TOP RIGHT: **Fig. 7.** The Triad block shows Alice's "hand-embroider quilting" stitches.

BOTTOM RIGHT: **Fig. 8.** The back of the Triad block shows the stitching that is part of the actual quilting of EBULLIENCE. Uneven stitches are part of this quilt's textural beauty.

Meet Alice Hobbs Parsons

Alice Hobbs Parsons is an artist whose work has been exhibited from coast to coast and is included in many private and corporate collections. Her artist's eye offers a unique but recognizable style when presented in her eclectic blending of fabrics, embellishments, and even rusty metal found objects. Her restraint is refreshing and eye-catching as she is unafraid to mix many media into her work.

When not quilting, she is involved in gardening, photography, and collage artistry. Other favorite activities are eating out, viewing movies, and travelling. She says, "I am very fortunate, love life, and I am never bored." Alice resides in Belmont, Maine, with artist Jerry, her lovable and very funny husband.

PHOTO: Jerry D. Parsons

EBULLIENCE, 48" x 60", made by Alice Hobbs Parsons

Jester

Jester, *12" x 12",* made by Susan Gerhardt

The Focus Block

App-expert Susan Gerhardt instructs us that for her construction of Jester, her focus block, raw-edge appliqué works best. Because that has been the method most often used by the app-experts, instead of hearing of Susan's technique, let's view her Jester block as it is being created.

Two factors influenced fabric and color choices. Having just worked on a quilt with shades of brown and beige, she needed a change. Jester looked happy, fun, and colorful.

Susan began her journey with an overall plan that she admits changed, so more decisions were made along the way (Fig. 1).

Fig. 1. Susan began by selecting an array of lights and darks in cool colors.
PHOTO: Susan Gerhardt

She machine satin stitched around all the appliqué pieces. She used some hand embroider to accent color and details using decorative threads.

Okay, time to go to work: trace design onto a stabilized background, trace pattern pieces onto fusible, do a rough layout of central crown motif. Try to not ponder too long. Be spontaneous.

Figs. 2 and 3. Compare the two different crowns—light yellow on the left and a darker cheddar on the right. Color spontaneity is important to maintain the fun of this block. PHOTOS: Susan Gerhardt

Here is a quick color change of the Jester's crown. The first one discarded was too pale. Susan kept the deeper cheddar crown (Figs 2 and 3).

As others have done, Susan began at the horizontal leaf section at the block's base (Fig. 4), stitching down the edges as she ironed any overlapping units. She tried not to overthink. The purple-raspberry under the black multidot is made of only one fabric. Nice touch.

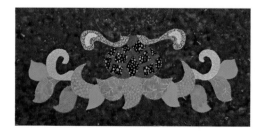

Fig. 4. Start of the leaf section
PHOTO: Susan Gerhardt

Watch as the block grows with more saturated colors, giving Jester dramatic flair and depth (Figs 5, 6, 7, and 8).

Details are important. The color harmony that Susan selected did not dominate over the designs. The striking and intense colors gave emphasis to each block. Without decorative stitching, Jester would have been flat, whereas adding it prior to quilting was a magic bridge to integrate art with appliqué (Fig. 9). More decorative stitchery was added during the quilting.

A Jester's reputation is a happy-go-lucky fellow who brings laughter, joy, and merriment wherever he goes.

Fig. 5. Red accents added to the crown PHOTO: Susan Gerhardt

Fig. 6. Yellow exterior added PHOTO: Susan Gerhardt

Fig. 7. Turquoise middle layered on top PHOTO: Susan Gerhardt

Fig. 8. All fabrics applied PHOTO: Susan Gerhardt

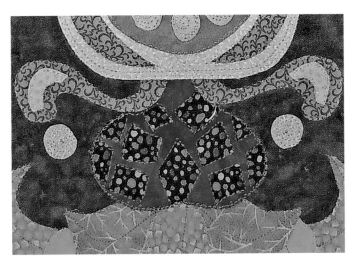

Fig. 9. A close-up shows the stitchery around parts of the applied pieces. PHOTO: Susan Gerhardt

Susan's Quilt

Each block of Susan's full-size quilt was quilted separately with a quilt-as-you-go technique. She selected AUDREY, TOO as the quilt's name and that story should be told.

Susan reveals that decisions for the app-project were not easy for her since it was different from anything she had ever done. Her dreams were invaded as she imagined leaves and greenery growing. Coincidentally, at the same time she was working on her quilt, is it any surprise that she saw a stage production of *Little Shop of Horrors*.

"If you are familiar with the plot line," said Susan, "there is a plant that begins to grow larger and larger." The famous line, *"Fe-e-e-e-ed ME!"* resounds. The plant needs to eat people to stay alive. Audrey II was the name given to the plant, after the lead character's love interest. Hmmmm, does that mean Audrey II, the quilt, ate her up?

The name, AUDREY, TOO, plays upon the twisted but funny production. We laugh with Susan at how the recurrence of dream leaves grew into a beautiful quilt with the blocks bound together with their repetition.

Meet Susan Gerhardt

Susan Gerhardt, a coast-of-Maine resident, began quilting about 20 years ago. She had a demanding 60-hour per week corporate job and stumbled into quilting, presently her passion, which got her through long work days.

She considers herself an art quilter and rarely uses anyone's patterns. Susan is a process person who loves to experiment, who wants to work as she goes, and ordinarily does not do detailed procedures.

She and her husband are owned by two cats who allow "their people" to serve as staff for them.

AUDREY, TOO, 38" x 50½", made by Susan Gerhardt

Lindy Loop

Lindy Loop, 12" x 12",
detail from Cirque du Quilt,
made by Ruth Ludwig Lind.
Full quilt on page 71.

Lindy Loop, 12" x 12",
detail from Dancing with Dianne,
made by Steven L. Carr.
Full quilt on page 62.

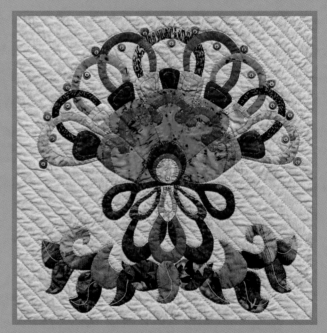

Lindy Loop, 12" x 12",
detail from Flower Baslket,
made by Glenna Graves Quigley.
Full quilt on page 22.

The Bonus Block

Lindy Loop is the only block that wasn't given as a focus block. It was designed as an afterthought for Ruth.

I truly wanted to name this block Loopy Lindy playing off of Ruth Lind's name, but thought she might not like it. Silly me. She laughed. The name was perfect in that it was Ruth who requested another block. She needed one more for her quilt layout. So, it is a reversal of my original block name: Lindy Loop; and loops it has—in mega numbers.

Seeing the three blocks together presents an interesting way to examine different techniques and interpretations. The comparison reinforces how you are permitted to interpret the designs for yourself and to recognize how easily the line-drawn block designs may be executed in different ways.

For example, pay attention to the base, the place where the five downward-directed loopy things sit on top of the three larger loops (Figs 1, 2,

and 3). Ruth and Glenna appliquéd loops directly onto backgrounds, making the loops similar to the larger ones below them, becoming another element in the "holder" of the larger fan loop.

Steve, however, saw it differently and inserted a pale aqua fabric underneath the loops; the additional fabric makes the two-part unit appear to be a part of the fan-loop. It's all in the eye and all three are viable, encouraged, and excellent interpretations.

There are lots of circular motifs in my designs. It goes without saying that often each app-expert applied dots in many different ways.

Dots, being a dominant design element in all of the 14 block designs, are shown here in three ways. Let's check out how each of these three experts fashioned dots.

Look at the ones that surround the largest loop area at the top of the motif (Figs. 4, 5, and 6, page 40). Steve raw-edge appliquéd his dots with a very neat buttonhole stitch.

Fig. 1. Ruth's five downward loops

Fig. 2. Glenna's five downward loops

Fig. 3. Steve's five downward loops

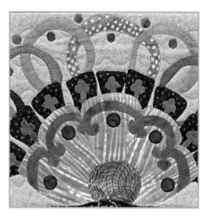

Fig. 4. Steve's dots on the large loop area

Fig. 5. Glenna's dots on the large loop area

Fig. 6. Ruth's dots on the large loop area

Glenna beautifully hand appliquéd the dots in place and added a gold metal bead for glimmer. The glitz that Ruth applied allowed triangular and circular Swarovski® crystals to replace fabric. All good. All.

Look at all the quilts to see other ways to place dots into a motif.

Still other notable differences include how each maker may have deleted certain elements. Glenna did not use the tiny triad unit in her alternating violet and lavender nine-fan motif. She also deleted the dots within the turquoise area.

In these three Lindy Loop blocks, modifications were freely made. The most dominant alteration is Glenna's enlargement of Lindy Loop to be the center medallion of her 13-block quilt (page 22). It makes me happy to see how such changes are easily made.

It is a fun exercise to do side-by-side comparisons of how each person changed the blocks for personal taste, implementation, ease of appli-

cation, skill, or whatever. Any of those is reason enough to make changes. Choose your own area for comparison.

You go for it in your own interpretation. If, at decision time, you find yourself stumped at what color, fabric, embellishment, or implementation might work for you, take a minute to enjoy a comparison of these app-experts' blocks. You might like their eye, their artistic sight. Without compromising the design, you might even find a way to blur the edges as many did when opting to change, substitute, or delete certain lines.

No matter how you make such alterations, the design remains; it may have the freshness of being simpler, or more complex. Often, it is decision time that is the most difficult part of a quilt's journey—the moment you pick up raw material (the fabric) and the line drawing (the block design), an interaction begins. It is a blending of imagination with fabric bits in color, texture, and scale. It is where you make your own bold design decisions.

Low Vase

Low Vase, 12" x 12", made by Janet E. Knapp
quilted by Loretta Pelletier, Topsham, Maine

The Focus Block

Right off the bat, Janet makes you smile with her quilt's name pun, KN-APP FOR HIRE (page 46). She playfully combined a portion of her last name, my last name, and the fact that we have jumped into an appliqué project together. Immediately, I knew Janet would be fun to have on board.

Here is Janet's plan to implement her focus block, Low Vase: hand needle-turn appliqué (her preferred method of working); some reverse appliqué; possibly embellishments with embroidery and/or buttons. All of that is accomplished in her block. "Low Vase, my feature block, and all the other blocks gave me a rather whimsical feeling with which I could have some fun."

Desiring a dark background, Janet first tried a solid black, then she auditioned several black-and-white prints (Figs. 1 and 2).

At the end, a mottled, dark burnt sienna was selected for the background. To allow for shrinkage from the stitchery, 14" x 14" squares were cut to receive the 12" x 12" block design.

Fig. 1. The prints that were mostly black disappeared into the flat solid black background. **PHOTO:** Janet E. Knapp

Fig. 2. The deep shade of maroon, almost burgundy, a complement on the color wheel to teal, appeared much better, but was discarded in the final cut. **PHOTO:** Janet E. Knapp

Janet's Technique

With fabrics prepared, Janet describes her technique.

1. I carefully numbered the pieces on the pattern in the sequence they would be appliquéd, starting with the back and working forward.

2. I traced the pieces onto freezer paper and numbered the pieces according to the pattern.

3. The 14" background square was marked with the pattern. I used a white transfer paper similar to carbon paper saved from a workshop several years ago. With this paper between the pattern and the background fabric with the white coated side on the background, I traced the pattern.

4. Now the fabric selection process really started for the individual elements of the block. All those circles started to taunt me. After looking over my black-and-white collection, I quickly determined I could let the fabric do the work in several places.

5. I found a white fabric printed with different sized black circles that worked well for the top back part of the appliqué. I then found a fabric with loops that looked similar to the loopy blossoms sitting in the vase, as well as fabrics that looked like leaves. (Don't be surprised if "let the fabric do the work" becomes a theme for this quilt!)

6. I used reverse appliqué for the circles in another section.

7. After cutting out the numbered freezer paper pieces, I ironed them *onto the top* of the fabrics and cut them out leaving ⅛"– ¼" to turn under. I finger pressed the margin to the back before appliquéing each piece and used silk thread and a straw needle for the appliqué. The actual appliqué progressed nicely.

8. Using a stem stitch, I embroidered the veins on the leaves with two strands of black embroidery floss. The accent lines on the vase and teal arch were done with two strands metallic silver thread.

9. I just had one element left: the small circles on top of the loopy blossoms. These were so tiny—too tiny for me to appliqué, and I found no fabric suitable to do the work. After two attempts with fabric, I tried buttons and settled on tiny white buttons sewn on with black thread. I'm not totally satisfied with these buttons, but they will be fine for now.

PHOTO: Janet E. Knapp

Fig. 3. The Piña block highlights the variety of fabrics used by Janet in her quilt. The silver threads reflect light.

Janet's Quilt

Janet's completed quilt is elegant and has an air of mystery and unpredictability. How I wish you could hold the quilt in your hands to appreciate her selected lustrous materials. There are sumptuous turquoise and teal fabrics, many are hand-dyed and painted fabrics from Diane Neil of Camden, Maine. Such a shimmering, watery blue palette is lush, almost iridescent. Silver threads, artistically applied around the hand-appliquéd units, brighten the mottled burnt sienna background (Fig. 3).

Chic black-and-white print fabric additions are a surprise. This contrasts Janet's traditional handcraft techniques with a sense of liberation, many of the fabrics being appropriate for the whimsical mood she sensed from the designs. There should be an APPLAUSE button right here so we could press it on her behalf. Hear, hear. Hear, hear.

Janet states that her first impressions of all the blocks were, "There's a lot going on here," and "Look at all those tiny circles!" Circles are her least favorite to appliqué. But, as we've already seen, those little round things can be worked in other ways.

Janet used silk thread to appliqué every single block; every single tiny motif was hand needle-turned. That, according to Janet, was the only traditional aspect of her stitching of KN—APP FOR HIRE.

Janet credits Margaret J. Miller's *Smashing Sets: Exciting Ways to Arrange Quilt Blocks* for inspiring the spiral settings.

Meet Janet E. Knapp

Janet E. Knapp, a true Mainer, grew up in West Paris. Later, she moved to Connecticut, working in various financial positions while earning an MBA. From her early years in a 4-H Club and high school, Janet's interest in needlework was piqued, but her introduction to quiltmaking was in West Hartford. After learning everything possible by hand, her next project was by machine. She was hooked and, needless to say, she hasn't pieced by hand since!

Returning to her home state with her husband over 20 years ago, she has continued with quilting; her skilled proficiency is evident to all. She enjoys books by Scandinavian suspense writers; and, "In another life," says Janet, "I would be a singer. I'd love to grab a microphone and sing my heart out! I'll do us all a favor and stick to quilting and reading."

PHOTO: Diane Neil

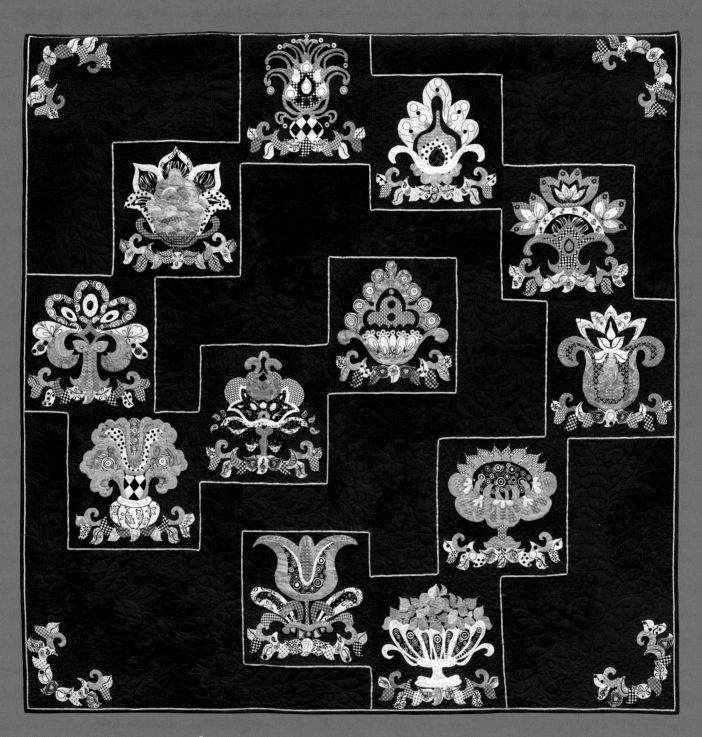

KN—APP FOR HIRE, 60" x 60", made by Janet E. Knapp
quilted by Loretta Pelletier, Topsham, Maine

Marbles

The completed satin-stitched Marbles block, 12" x 12", made by Roxannne (Rocky) Wells

Fig. 1. Marbles drawn onto freezer paper, awaiting application to fabrics **PHOTO:** Roxanne Wells

Fig. 2. Freezer paper is laid upon fabric, but not ironed.
PHOTO: Roxanne Wells

Fig. 3. Place parchment paper on top of freezer paper motif, and then iron. **PHOTO:** Roxanne Wells

The Focus Block

Rocky's favored method is satin-stitch appliqué. The first step is to draw the pattern onto freezer paper (Fig. 1).

Cut out all the individual pattern units from the freezer paper and iron onto the wrong side of the selected fabrics. If you do not like the fabric selected, remove the freezer paper pattern and re-iron onto another fabric.

Rocky's Hints for Satin-Stitch Appliqué

❊ For a stabilizer, wad a second sheet of freezer paper, smooth it out, and iron it to the back of the completely fused block. It comes off more easily due to the wadded wrinkle lines. The freezer paper acts as a slider, easing the block through the machine when satin stitching.

❊ No doubt you will gum up your iron's surface at some point. I LOVE Dritz® Iron-Off Hot Iron Cleaner.

❊ Practice satin stitching by testing the width and tightness before you start on your original block.

❊ Two solutions for a bit of bad stitchery: pick it out or cover it over with a second, wider line of stitching.

❊ Lay a piece of kitchen parchment paper over the freezer paper when applying it to fabric and then iron. It prevents gunking up your iron (Figs. 2 and 3).

Watch as the progression of added little portions create Rocky's Marbles block (Figs. 4, 5, and 6, page 49).

Fig. 4. PHOTO: Roxanne Wells

Fig. 5. PHOTO: Roxanne Wells

Fig. 6. PHOTO: Roxanne Wells

Rocky's Quilt

Rocky met the 12-block appliqué challenge head on. Her decision to make the designs her own while maintaining the blocks' integrity resulted in her quilt, HIGH ANXIETY (page 52). Her plan: incorporate the 12 blocks into a four-panel wallhanging by merging several blocks into each other. Three of the presented line drawn designs were overlaid to construct a single ornate flower face stemming from a small pot. Rocky's unique presentation offers new meaning to the designs. Well done. As you see, there are many ways to use the blocks. It will be a joy to see how you recreate the design.

Of late, her appliqué tools are her sewing machine and fusible backing; she prefers the neat finished edge that satin stitching produces. This also gives the quilt enough sturdiness to hold up under the duress of multiple washings.

A batik's tightly woven threads help eradicate fraying and splitting along your stitching edge. If you are using a more loosely woven fabric, fraying may occur. Try either Krylon® Spray Adhesive on the back of unit to be appliquéd or apply a thin bead of Sobo® Premium Craft and Fabric Glue on the edges of a unit (white glue in a tube; it dries clear).

Rocky selected batiks in two colorways (Figs. 7 and 8).

Fig. 7. PHOTO: Roxanne Wells

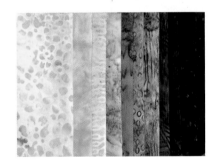

Fig. 8. PHOTO: Roxanne Wells

Fig. 9. The Sunflower and Fleur de Lis blocks are combined. Note how Fleur de Lis holds up Sunflower and appears to be foliage.

For fusing onto the background, iron Steam A Seam® fusible to the backside of the batiks. Lay freezer paper (shiny side down) on top of the line drawing and precisely trace the design using a light box. "Freezer paper is an extremely necessary item," asserts Rocky, who uses it for both drawing the design and as a stabilizer.

An interesting thing occurred during the fusion of the 12 blocks. When the four flowers were finished, Rocky admits that her focus block, Marbles, became less significant than others. Instead of it being the stand-out block, it evolved into the flower pot for housing the cleverly dramatic Sunflower – Fleur de Lis combination block (Fig. 9). What a terrific idea—combining two blocks into a new one. You try it.

Meet Roxanne Wells

PHOTO: John Wells

Roxanne (Rocky) Wells came to quilting in much the same way as did many of us Mainers who are "from away." She pursued a business career and grew up in a small Midwest farm town where her roots remain. Today she proudly announces, "I have my feet firmly planted in the dirt," a fact evident in her love for colorful perennial gardening.

She has been quilting for about 10 years, initially sticking to tried and true traditional patterns, but quickly moving to less structured methods. "Following precise directions and carefully sewing a straight line didn't work for me. So I went with what I refer to as the 'just wing it' approach to quilting."

"I now have the confidence to let the creative process follow its own path," she says, "and I can get as whacky and colorful and creative as I want." That says it all.

Only one design had to be turned upside down.

For finishing touches, the four panels were joined with a lacy metallic ribbon and dangling leaves of fused double-sided batiks. The panels appear to be hanging from a twisted golden rope, the rope covered with the same ribbon.

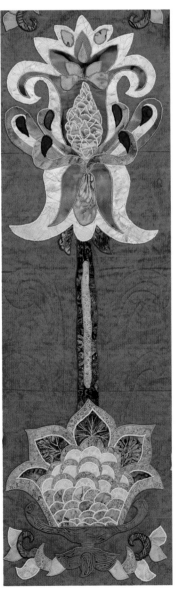

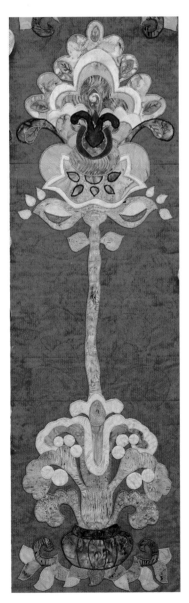

Fig. 10. Jester/Triad combined (at the top) over Philodendron

Fig. 11. Piña/Tulip combined (at the top) over Clamshell

Fig. 12. Low Vase/Harp combined (at the top) over Feathers II

HIGH ANXIETY, 50" x 48½", made by Roxanne Wells

Philodendron

Philodendron, 12" x 12", made by Gail Galloway-Nicholson

Fig. 1. This is the first fabric choice. Pewter is a favorite color of Gail's.
PHOTO: Diane Neil

Fig. 2. First Philodendron block placed on the back of the quilt
PHOTO: Diane Neil

The Focus Block

Gail Galloway-Nicholson quickly made an executive color decision: to go quietly into this project. During the process of making her focus block, Philodendron, Gail saw herself veering toward a brighter palette, but instead, held back, listened to her design voice, and stayed quietly soft.

Several fabrics were considered at first, including magenta hand-dyed gradations, for the bowl, view a Japanese tone-on-tone pewter-colored print, for the many leaves, see the gradations of green, a blue-green print, and one printed fabric (Fig. 1).

Not only did the magenta gradations get edited out, the first Philodendron block she created was eliminated. She placed it in the center of the back of her quilt (Figs. 2–3).

Look carefully at the print fabric behind the looped bowl. It is no longer in her palette. Her luxurious cluster beading with large, mottled blue beads is extremely sophisticated and opulent.

Initially, the entire Philodendron block was more vibrant and had many violet-and-green beads in the leaves, but they were replaced with blue ones (Fig. 3). This was no longer the quiet look Gail had planned, she preferred the calming colors of Maine.

Fig. 3. Gail's first finished Philodendron, her focus block **PHOTO:** Diane Neil

Gail began again, feeling that her original was not soft enough for the quilt she wanted to create.

The new block has a totally different and unique look. The colors are more contained—fewer gradations of green, simplified and sleek. You see from the previous edited-out block and from those following that Gail is an accomplished decorative beader. Her beading adds intricacy, giving a lavish look to her two beaded blocks, Sunflower (Fig. 4) and Philodendron (Fig. 5).

Fig. 4. Sunflower, one of two beaded blocks

Gail's Quilt

The quilt is a classic masterpiece. A deliciously intense water-blue fabric was selected for the background. Restraint is sometimes refreshing, often yielding a quilt of modest finesse and such must be said of Gail's quilt, Mainely Blue and Green, page 57. The sapphire blue glows; it is subtle, yet speaks vibrantly.

The machine quilting was done by Julie Stegna of Walpole, Maine. All of the appliqué, embroidery, and beading is done by Gail's hand. She uses freezer paper for the appliqué.

Gail leaves us with an original poem.

Fig. 5. The finished Philodendron block as it appears in Gail's quilt

Mainely Blue and Green–Aren't We Lucky to Live on the Coast of Maine?
Green are the hills and the gardens that abound.
Green, the needles of the trees that surround.
Blue are the lakes and the Penobscot Bay.
Blue, the sky that brightens my day.

PHOTO: Diane Neil

Meet Gail Galloway-Nicholson

Gail Galloway-Nicholson, a transplant from Pennsylvania by way of Virginia, maintains that her 30-year job was the most exciting in the world, Curator of the United States Supreme Court.

No one in Gail's family had an interest in the needle arts, so quilt DNA was not present. She became spellbound watching a lady work with bits of fabric at a monthly auction. Still employed in DC, Gail got up at 4:30 a.m. to quilt before going to work, sewing on an old Singer machine given to her when she was 16.

Retiring about 10 years ago, Gail now spends her days quilting, oil painting, gardening, and enjoying nature at its best in Maine.

MAINELY BLUE AND GREEN, 46½" x 59", made by Gail Galloway-Nicholson

Piña

PIÑA, 12" x 12", made by Steven L. Carr

The Focus Block

Buttonhole appliqué with a micro-blanket stitch over raw edges is Steven L. Carr's favorite way to appliqué, noting that a myriad of effects can be created based on choice of thread color. Steve accomplishes the neatest, cleanest appliqué I've ever seen. The work more closely resembles needle-turn than raw-edge appliqué.

The process to create such excellence is freely revealed by Steven. "My technique is to stitch as I go." In fact, such a method eliminates several steps along the way. Not only does he stitch each component in the design as he goes, he also uses a "quilt-as-you-go" technique, and doesn't use a light box.

Steven's Technique

You'll need vellum (a translucent parchment), or a clear plastic sheet for a placement guide.

Background Sandwiching and Quilting

1. Cut a background and a backing fabric; sandwich with batting. All three must be cut larger than the finished block size. For the 12" x 12" finished block, begin with 14½" x 14½" squares. Quilt through all three layers. For simplicity, Steve uses an undulating horizontal quilting stitch (Fig. 1).

2. Place the block pattern right-side up and overlay with vellum (or clear vinyl); trace the outlines of the design using a Sharpie® Fine Point marker. You're making a fabric placement guide (Fig. 2).

3. Audition and assemble your fabrics.

4. To skip the need for a light box, first trace the shapes for one fabric at a time onto a fusible such as Lite Steam-A-Seam 2® from the original Piña block design, with the design right-side up. Use a **brown** Sharpie Ultra-Fine Point marker. One fabric at a time helps to stay organized.

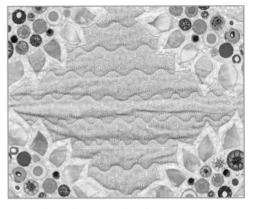

Fig. 1. Three layer sandwich is quilted with a simple curvy-motion horizontal stitch. This is the first step toward neatly appliquéd quilts a lá Steve Carr.

Fig. 2. A traced Vellum paper guide is critical in an elaborate design such as Piña. PHOTO: Steven L. Carr

Fig. 3. Under the presser foot is a tiny brown unit ready to be sewn onto the already quilted cross-hatched yellow base of the pineapple, showing Steve's quilt-as-you-go method. PHOTO: Steven L. Carr

5. Now, get any plain white sheet of paper and turn the fusible over and trace over the already drawn shapes using a different color Sharpie marker. Why use two colors? Steve notes "I draw the original in brown to remind myself that the brown side stays down when placed on the actual fabric." Since this particular fusible may be adhered from either side, he coined this little device to be sure to use the right side: **Brown** = Down. Neat Trick.

6. Fuse the shapes to the various fabrics and cut out your appliqués, with the exception of the yellow base (see step 8), cutting on the drawn line. When cutting many small pieces, be sure to number them; corral them into some kind of small container as you cut them out so each piece may be correctly sorted, retrieved, and applied.

Placement

A key to successfully build Piña is to take some time to review which unit must be overlaid onto another. Instead of applying several units with the fusible, only apply one unit, then appliqué that piece into place.

7. Use the see-through design template you created in Step 2. Mark the center of the design and the center of the block's background; match up the center point. Make sure the design is straight with respect to the edges of the block. Pin the placement guide to the top of the background block.

8. Position your yellow base pineapple underneath the guide. The yellow is purposefully cut oversized so that the outer scales (units) hold it down when sewn. The diagonal cross-hatched stitchery is quilted onto yellow Piña base before applying any other units (Fig. 3, page 59); thus, this background is quilted as you go. You also see the first upright unit for the Piña's midsection.

9. When you are ready to adhere the fusible to the yellow fabric, go ahead and peel off the backing (the side with the **brown** drawing) but be sure that the adhesive film stays attached to the other side (the one with the other color-drawn design). Place on the fabric and iron briefly; do NOT use steam. Alternatively, you can use a dab of Roxanne Glue-Baste-It.

Machine Stitching

10. For the buttonhole stitch, use a size 60 needle to minimize the appearance of holes. Use 50 wt. thread in the bobbin. Try out machine settings to find what works best for you. Set your buttonhole stitch width and length to 1.0 or 1.5mm, the tightest setting for your machine. This accomplishes two things: it keeps the bobbin thread from being pulled to the top of the quilt and it creates a trapunto-like effect when the design is complete.

11. Begin sewing the pieces of the center pineapple. Numbering the pieces of the design and pieces of fabric helps to stay organized. Start at the top of the motif; sew down the first piece (Fig. 4, page 61). Watch a spot slightly ahead of the needle instead of watching the needle as it enters the fabric.

12. Continue sewing the pineapple pieces row by row, alternating: left side piece(s), right-side piece(s), and then middle piece(s) before moving down to the next row (Fig. 5). (The center is the multicolored brown/navy/gold/purple motif.)

13. Sew down the outer arms of the pineapple.

14. Sew the upper leaves starting at the top and moving down to the pineapple from outside to inside. The teardrop shape that matches the center pineapple is the last one to get sewn down.

15. Finally, sew the festoon of leaves below the pineapple. I sewed the outside left, then the outside right, one at a time, moving towards the center (Fig.6).

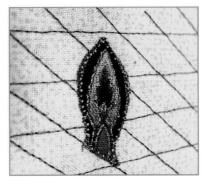

Fig. 4. Sewing the first and top piece of the pineapple motif
PHOTO: Steven L. Carr

Fig. 5. Top, left, right, middle—four units sewn onto already quilted yellow background, the beginning of the central pineapple motif
PHOTO: Steven L. Carr

Steve's Quilt

f I were handing out awards, Steve's quilt, Dancing with Dianne, page 63, would easily receive three:

Most Literal Interpretation of Designs: So far, I haven't found one design that Steve did not follow to the letter. His ability to machine stitch around tiny dots (Fleur de Lis, third block down in the left column), miniature ovals (Triad, second block down in the right column), and petite curves (Clamshell, second block down in the left column) is remarkable.

Best Manicured: There are no frays, no loose threads, no unkempt areas on Steve's quilt. That, he explains, is by the use of the micro-blanket stitch. I cannot wait to use this technique on my next piece.

Fig. 6. Piña is complete and ready to be assembled into the final quilt.

DANCING WITH DIANNE, 71½" x 72", made by Steven L. Carr

Surprise Dianne by Using a Discarded Block: Yes, there were several designs that were discarded; and yes, Steve blindsided me when, during that last week before the manuscript and quilts were due at the publisher, I spent an overload of time comparing each quilt with information–dotting all those pesky i's and making sure all those t's were crossed; and, there it was—a fourteenth block, Feathers I (Fig. 7).

I originally discarded the design for Feathers I. The line drawing had way too many ditsy little things, if you ask me. But Steve liked the challenge. The detail shows (what else?) *detail* and lots of it. I laugh as I write, of course. Thus, because of Steve's inclusion, a copy of Feathers I is available in the Coloring Book Gallery section.

Fig. 7. Feathers I, DANCING WITH DIANNE, detail

Meet Steven L. Carr

Steven L. Carr is a librarian by profession and an enthusiastic quilter who once owned a quilt shop in Pennsylvania where he lives.

Well known for his extraordinary skill at choosing colors and his texture and hue combinations, he once was seen discussing fabric choices with his friend, Teresa. Nothing strange about that, you say. Well, no, not usually. It was just that they were sitting underneath a table and exchanging fabrics that were spilling everywhere.

It was then I knew we all would be good buds.

PHOTO: John Conroy, Jr.

Piña in Wool

RECALCITRANT HUMILITY, 34" x 38", made Judy Roche

The Focus Block Quilt

Around here, if you combine the words "antique, heirloom, and quilts," immediately Judy Roche comes to mind. Her extensive collection and her historical knowledge about quilts and quilt-making gives rise to how she approached the design of Piña. She reimagined the pineapple, took the simple line drawing and, without any design barriers, made it spectacularly classic. Not only did Judy enlarge the design making it four times the original, she also took on the challenge of creating it in wool. Her three-dimensional quilt is a classic mix of refined appliqué but with an updated twist.

The wool edges are left without any confines of stitchery. View how that presents an incredible harmonious blending of textural rough wool with a more contemporary design interpretation, opulent, but includes old-fashioned elegance in keeping with Judy's bent toward traditional quilts.

The central area has embroidered yellow verticals applied sequentially, in much the same manner as other app-experts. Look carefully at each stitched petal; look at the nubby surface of the upright corrugated background that appears as if it were channel stitched; view the variety gathered for the darker, richly-colored exterior petals that contain the central area. An eclectic mix of plaids, herringbones, checks, and hand-dyed solids were all incorporated for a heightened sensory wooliness (Fig. 1).

Colorways range from celadon to olive to forest, golden yellow to ochre to touches of chocolate, and every shade within these palettes. Certainly, an almost old-fashioned coloring, but Piña, as offered with its edgy construction, is anything but old fashioned.

Judy meticulously underscores the versatility of colonial knots,

Fig. 1. The highly textured surface adds a breath of new life to the design.

Fig. 2. More texture, handcrafted and embroidered to perfection, is added via colonial knots.

placing them all along the green leaf foundation below the Piña (Fig. 2). She drops more knots above the leafy crown. Even more knots bring depth and emphasis to the pale olive center of each of the two curved leaves at the side, dotting them with dimension.

This brings ups a question to you, the reader: If wool is a viable source for an enlarged block, why not linen? How about jute? And silk? What about leather or suede? Endless are the possibilities should you dare to be different and try new ways. You have been given permission. You have the freedom to create. There is room for more ideas—yours!

Meet Judy Roche

Judy Roche ordered her first quilt pattern in 1961 and life became a chain reaction. Her extensive repertoire includes quilting, restoration of old quilts, writing about quilts, studying quilts and the history of quilts, collecting nineteenth century quilts, curating museum exhibits, designing quilt patterns, judging, teaching, lecturing on vintage quilts, and even working with fabric companies, helping to produce historically accurate reproduction fabrics.

During this time she traveled all over, but the best part, says Judy, "is all the quilters I have met and befriended over the years—a very special group of people."

Judy continues her on-going education about quilts—from every single quilter she has met, in every place she has lived, and each class, seminar, and conference she has attended, because history is still being written for Judy Roche.

Sunflower

Sunflower, 12" x 12", made by Ruth Ludwig Lind

Ruth's Quilt

By now you know that each app-expert furnished information about his or her particular focus block and quilt. When I pressed Ruth to give me more information about her quilt, here is what she sent me. No way could it be better told, nor any funnier.

About the quilt in her own words:

Not that many years ago, I avoided appliqué like I avoided the vacuum cleaner. I always figured if you wanted flowers all over your quilt, you should just buy flowered fabric! But a historical quilt guild I belonged to was making an appliquéd quilt one year, and I either had to learn how or quit the guild.

These precious ancient ladies insisted on the most cumbersome methods possible, cutting out each piece, using cardboard templates, basting the precise 3/16" turn-unders, ironing each petal, basting it on the fabric, blah, blah, blah. There had to be a better way.

After years of reading books, taking classes, and experimenting, I stopped by my friend Judy Roche's house here in Maine on my motorcycle one October afternoon, quilting stuff in the saddlebag, as always. Among the group stitching and sipping tea that day was Jeana Kimball, who introduced me to back-basting appliqué. Oh. My. Gosh.

Fast forward to the app-project and line drawings. I had just finished a wallhanging for a friend, which for some odd reason I created in black and white. It never felt totally finished to me, at least as far as exploring the black-and-white theme. Dianne's designs screamed to me of black and white and silver, and BLING! She told me to have at it.

Near the beginning of the project, we traveled to South Carolina to visit my husband David's son and his family, who happened to have tickets to Cirque du Soleil®. Watching that spellbinding performance with a thousand things going on all at once—the odd and addicting music, dance, comedy, and gymnastics—total art in its highest form—crystallized in my mind what this quilt needed to be.

I worked on the blocks sort of all at once, back basting and embellishing upstairs in the sewing room by day, needle-turning in front of trashy television at night. The hand quilting wasn't quite the joyful process that crafting the blocks had been. Because of the thousands of crystals and delicate metallic thread embroidery, I needed to use a frame, which meant hours and hours sitting in one position, working with the challenging Mylar® and metallic threads the design demanded. But done is done, and I even still like CIRQUE DU QUILT.

Now, all I have to learn is to step away from the black-and-white fabrics whenever I go into a quilt shop!

A Unique Delivery

CIRQUE DU QUILT was hand delivered to the author by way of "Muriel," Ruth's Ural Sidecar Motorcyle. It wasn't long before Ruth pushed me into taking my first ride. Helmeted, we both resembled strange alien bugs, but the ride is fabutantastic (Fig. 1).

What more can I say? Ruth Lind has paid attention to all the details. The quilt is pristine in its monochromatic black-white-gray-silver lack of color, a true knock out within a repetitive frame, and has the most seriously awesome appliqué imaginable. The interaction of sparkly bling, the sizzle of shining rhinestones, clear glass beads, tiny black jet dots, Swarovski crystals, and even silver braiding here and there all make CIRQUE DU QUILT the most striking of quilts.

Ruth, with lavish chic style, has mixed traditional needle-turn appliqué with a more contemporary look. She has reached out to explore and to encounter new ways of seeing. I can only say "Bravo, dear friend, bravo." Bravo especially for using various kinds and types of metallic threads for the hand quilting and embroidery.

Enjoy a close-up view of some of the blocks in Ruth's CIRQUE DU QUILT.

Fig. 1. Yes, this is how Ruth delivered the magnificent CIRQUE DU QUILT.

Row 1, 1st block: Fleur de Lis

Row 1, 2nd block: Piña

Row 2, 1st block: Low Vase

Row 2, 2nd block: Tulip

Row 4, 1st block: Feathers II

Row 4, 2nd block: Triad

PHOTO: David A. Lind

Meet Ruth Ludwig Lind

Somewhere around the age of five, and as soon as her mother would let her hold a needle, Ruth Ludwig Lind began sewing. Many years of garment and home dec sewing ensued but it was in 1987 she took up quilting and hasn't looked back since.

Mr. Lind, her treasured and beloved husband, finally found her over the Internet many years later, and her first valentine to him was a quilt.

In Maine, she headed up a quilt drive, gathering, and shipping over 200 quilts to Christchurch, New Zealand, after the tragic earthquake of February 2011.

A hot air and gas balloon pilot since 1979, Ruth eventually fell in love with her husband's passion for motorcycles and learned how to ride. The Linds travel each year to someplace very far away, rent two bikes, and explore. In addition to her BMWs, she also rides a quirky Ural with a sidecar named Muriel that sports Moxie® livery.

The Linds share their home with three dogs, three cats, and a rotating roster of foster kittens. All the animals insist on supervising the construction of each quilt.

CIRQUE DU QUILT, 63" x 78½", made by Ruth Ludwig Lind

Sunflower

Sunflower blocks with the appliqué set on point; each 12" x 12", made by Steven L. Carr

The Focus Block

The center of Steve Carr's quilt, DANCING WITH DIANNE (page 63) is composed of not one, but four Sunflower blocks that are provide a flourish of yellow.

Take a look at the detail of the Sunflower line drawing, same as furnished to all the app-experts. Observe the intricate overlays in the center. Take note of the circular seeds, itsy-bitsy circles drawn within tiny circles. Now, compare the line drawings (Fig 1) with the center of Steve's blocks (Fig 2).

What would you have done? I guess the answer to that question is the same thing I would have done and as did several of the app-experts: used fabrics that already had dots within dots—a work-around that needs only to be thought about with a slight brain twitch. If need be, find a different creative way.

Such a device is welcomed. Examples from other app-experts include using beads (Glenna's quilt, page 22; Gail's Sunflower block, page 55 and her quilt page 57) and fabrics (Arlaine's Sunflower block, page 26 and her quilt, page 27; Susan's quilt, page 37; Janet's quilt, page 46; Alice's Sunflower block page 30 and her quilt, page 32; and Rocky's Sunflower block page 50 and her quilt, page 52). Use your imagination; find a work-around for the line-drawn circles if you do not want to appliqué those miniscule round shapes. Artistic freedom. You have a creative license to enjoy.

Fig. 1. Detail of line drawn Sunflower block with dots within dots

Fig. 2. See how Steve's fabric creates tiny seed replicas.

Triad

Triad, 12" x 12", made by Susanne C. Rivers

The Focus Block

By substituting embroidery at certain points, Susanne C. Rivers artistically completed her Triad design. Often, Sue did a work-around using well executed decorative embroidery stitchery. Delicate lines, skillfully applied, make this a remarkable interpretation of the Triad line drawing.

Sue simplified the implied fabric layers that were assumed to be appliquéd; her creative eye reduced the design to its essence. She accomplished the block differently; the way Sue saw it, lines can be threads and motifs can be reinvented.

Sue shares her process with step-by-step instructions.

1. Photocopy the pattern and number each appliqué piece (Fig. 1).

2. Trace the design onto freezer paper. Because the bottom leaves are mirror images, save time by tracing only one side then fold the freezer paper in half, shiny sides together, and cut out both sides at the same time (Fig. 2).

3. Press freezer paper onto the RIGHT sides of leaf fabrics. For the chartreuse curly units, the upturned designs at the edge, press the freezer paper onto the WRONG side of the fabric. Secure the edges with Elmer's® All Purpose School Glue Stick.

4. Cut out a square for the background; mark registration lines with a sliver of soap.

5. Attach leaves to the background with a dot of the glue stick.

6. Appliqué starting from the outside leaves and work toward the center using a needle-turn technique (Fig. 3).

Fig. 1. Photocopied and numbered pattern PHOTO: Susanne C. Rivers

Fig. 2. Freezer-paper cutouts are placed upon the original design, ready to put onto fabric. PHOTO: Susanne C. Rivers

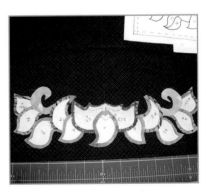

Fig. 3. The array of leaves prepared for appliquéing PHOTO: Susanne C. Rivers

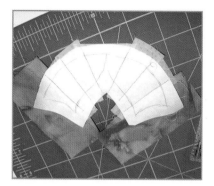

Fig. 4. Paper-pieced sunburst unit
PHOTO: Susanne C. Rivers

Fig. 5. Freezer paper is applied to the crown and magenta central motif. **PHOTO:** Susanne C. Rivers

Fig. 6. Almost finished
PHOTO: Susanne C. Rivers

7. An easy way to interpret an array of fabrics in rows like the yellow sunburst is to paper piece (Fig. 4). The unit is ready to cut around, leaving fabric to fold under in preparation for appliquéing. How easy is that?

8. Freezer paper is ironed onto the magenta area, as it is on the green half circle above the yellow sunburst, in preparation to appliqué. See how the paper-pieced sunburst so beautifully falls into place under the green crown (Fig. 5).

9. The final Triad sits on top of the design waiting to be appliquéd onto the background (Fig. 6).

10. Instead of appliquéing many of the smaller pieces, why not embroider the shapes? Sue used one or two strands of embroidery floss for a stem stitch. Circles were embroidered with a small blanket stitch and French knots were applied with two strands of floss wrapped four times.

To quote Sue, "With encouragement, I took liberties with the design." Yes, she did, and aren't we pleased to view her amazing creativity?

Susanne's Quilt

Susanne's outstanding quilt is a fine example of her expertise using classic needle-turn appliqué by hand. A warm blackened rust Thimbleberries® fabric, viewed as brown, is the background for her four-block quilt, DÉJÀ VU. Her love for bright colors often supersedes any use of more demure ones. Here, she combined a sedate brown with glowing green, chartreuse, lemon, orange, red, fuchsia, and every hue possible in-between for a dazzling color surprise. Finding ways to combine such colors is evident in Sue's works.

For fabrics, pay attention to the combinations of types. The background is a Thimbleberries® fabric considered a little bit country. In contrast, only intensely colored batiks are used for the appliqué. Sue chose batiks for the concentrated color and for the tighter weave that keeps the pieces from fraying during the appliqué process.

Meet Susanne C. Rivers

Susanne C. Rivers, from Searsport, Maine, is an accomplished quiltmaker whose style continues to refresh the art of needlework. Often, her unexpected and unpredictable color variations are not only striking, but are fine examples of design interpretation.

Laughing, she says about herself, "I began quilting years before the rotary cutter was invented." Intending to enroll in an adult education cake decorating class one night, a quilting instructor pleaded with her to take quilting instead. One more student was needed to keep from cancelling the class.

Sue creates samples for Simplicity Creative Group and receives fabric and new quilting tools from them. Hopefully, one of those packages included a rotary cutter.

PHOTO: Terry Hire

DÉJÀ VU, 37" x 37", made by Susanne C. Rivers

Tulip

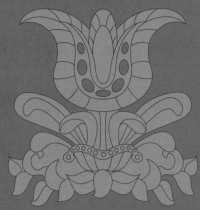

Tulip, *12" x 12", made by Patricia Burns*

The Focus Block

Patricia Burns is an appliqué perfectionist. Meticulous stitchery, a flair for color composition, and always striving for the best—those are Pat's appliqué ethics. The same exceptional traits and principles made working on the Tulip design a challenge for her, citing the combination of the piece sizes and their intricacies as the culprits testing her tenacity. She braved the challenge and dared to jump into the adventure.

Pat dismissed the technique of raw-edge appliqué with invisible quilting thread. Although she maintains it is neat and accurate, she did not want a full quilt made that way. She settled upon a back basting method a lá Jeana Kimball (Figs. 1 and 2).

For more about Jeana Kimball's technique as used by Glenna, Ruth, Susanne, and Pat, see "Back Basting Appliqué," *American Quilter* magazine, January 2009, pages 26–28.

For the Tulip block, Pat selected several colors for the leaves (Fig. 3), deep oranges and reds for the tulip, and pale brown for the vessel. A buff-colored backdrop is a perfect recipient for all these colors.

Pat constructed the tulip shape off block, meaning that it was created without being attached to the background or with the units layered sequentially to the background. It is easier to construct the entire Tulip separately, then back baste the larger shape in preparation for appliqué.

When called for, Pat also used a freezer paper method for some areas. Sometimes it is by trial and error, with a combination of methods—back basting, freezer paper, and off-block construction—that a good quality turned-edge appliqué may be achieved. That is Pat's way. She drew on her reservoir of talent and skill to make the designs, as can you.

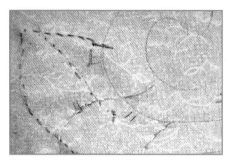

Fig. 1. Designs are basted in place from the back along pencil lines. The white threads show the basting done on the back of the block, whereas the green stitches show where Pat had already appliquéd one of the leaves. **PHOTO:** Patricia Burns

Fig. 2. Here, you can see the front of the block at the same stage—the front basting in white and the two-tone leaf appliquéd with matching green. **PHOTO:** Patricia Burns

Fig. 3. Depth and variety is accomplished by the use of fabrics such as geometrics in stripes and dots, semisolids, and miniprints. **PHOTO:** Patricia Burns

Pat's Quilt

There is no disputing this quilt is dynamic!

The finished quilt is a pristine example of handwork. The appliqué and quilting leave us wanting more—we want to sit beside Pat and watch as fingers stitch with her straightforward techniques, methods she generously shares.

For the background, she selected a neutral beige with a mini floral design that sets off the variety of mostly clear bright colors— turquoises, hot pinks, lilacs, blues, and yellows. That is how she took it from being ordinary to way beyond extraordinary. Perhaps you might say it is sumptuously elaborate. Pat's exact placement of green leaves in all blocks support her design knowledge that such repetition is glue to bring all the blocks together, as does the green ⅝" connecting sashing.

For your enjoyment, look at five more of Pat's blocks that were appliquéd before joined into the quilt top.

Piña

Sunflower

Jester

Low Vase

Marbles

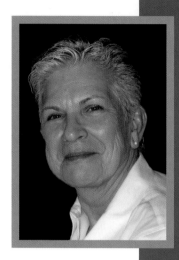

Meet Patricia Burns

Quilts, their colors, and their designs have always amazed and attracted Patricia C. Burns. In her thirties, while working, raising a family, and completing a bachelor's degree, she took her first quilting class. Pat drew her own templates, cut fabric with scissors, marked all the sewing lines, and constructed–what else?–a sampler. During this time, she yearned to make quilts but did not have the time for such a labor-intensive activity. By the year 2000, with fewer life commitments, she joined a quilt guild in New Jersey and never looked back.

Pat sees designs in European church floors, color combos in magazines, and inspirations in pieces of fabric. She sees endless ideas and choices. Quilting is an integral part of Pat's life. She says, "It's a very good part."

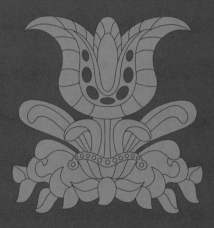

THE QUILT—A LIFE OF ITS OWN AND MINE, 61" x 78", made by Patricia Burns

RESOLUTION FOR FOUR, 53½" x 53½", made by Sabra Andersen

The Focus Blocks

Imagine my surprise when a little mouse told of Sabra Andersen's striking quilt featuring the Tulip (upper left), Triad (lower right), Low Vase (lower left), Marbles (upper right), and Harp (center) blocks. She describes them as a joy to create. She didn't, however, enjoy hand piecing the four Carpenter's Wheel blocks.

Her deep burgundy, olive green, and cream "pieced orphans" found a home when offset with the appliquéd blocks. By using the same color combinations, then adding to the palette—azalea pink, murky gold, and shades of lavender—she accomplished wonderful color interest.

Ordinarily, such a truly matched palette, including the border fabric, will often not have such excitement as you see in Sabra's quilt. It was her use of a dear friend's fabulous striped fabric that offers the eye delight. She achieves tension with the stripe's placement in angled positions instead of horizontal or vertical. Movement is created when your eye travels along the stripe's surface.

Note how Sabra brings the design element of repetition to the table with her own leaf arrangements in the border and corners. The quilt is absolutely beautiful. We are happy to present it to you.

Triad: Azalea pink, murky gold, and shades of lavender add excitement to a simple color palette of burgundy and olive.

Marbles: It is the striped fabric that makes one look and look again.

Sabra took the leaf designs and created her own combinations for the midpoint of her quilt and for the corners.

Meet Sabra Andersen

Sabra is another quiltmaker who learned needlework and clothing construction from her grandmother. She retired in 2007 after 33 years in molecular biology research. That's when the quilting bug bit. She purchased a long arm machine and is busy attaining a new skill. She lives in Belfast, Maine with her best friend, a white Akita named Sumo.

PHOTO: Terry Hire

Meet Robin Strobel

Robin Strobel was definitely a process person. Depending on her mood, she liked to call herself either a dilettante or a Renaissance woman. She was always looking to learn something new and seldom created the same thing the same way twice.

*She was passionate about a range of diverse topics. Robin worked with Martingale as an illustrator, technical editor, and author of two books (*The Casual Quilter *and* Quilter's Bounty*). She worked in quilt shops and taught quilting and fabric dyeing. She curated the How to Quilt section of ShopMartingale.com and wrote for the Stitch This! blog after she retired.*

Robin died in December 2012 and is fondly remembered by her many friends and colleagues.

PHOTO: Brent Kane

HOW TO RESIZE BLOCKS

According to quiltmaker and author Robin Strobel, to change the size of a quilt block, "Ya start with whatcha want, and ya divide it by whatcha got." Truly, how easy is that?

Robin's Instructions— In Her Own Words

Imagine a darling little appliqué that's just perfect for your wall, but the 12" x 12" block is too large. You decide you'd like to make it 10" x 10". You take the 12" pattern to a photocopier with the intent to make it smaller, but what percentage should you make it? "Ya start with whatcha want, and ya divide it by whatcha got."

Begin with your goal—it's the reason you have to deal with quilt math in the first place. What you want is a 10" block, so punch 10 into your calculator first. Hit the division key, then enter the number "ya got," which is 12. Press the = key. The number 0.83333333333 pops up.

The copy machine wants a percentage, so move that pesky decimal point two spots right, and then you're done (0.83333333333 to 83.33333333). Because this is a quilt, not a suspension bridge, you don't need all of the decimal points, so ignore them. You need to reduce the 12" pattern by 83% to make a 10" block. Yes, it's that easy to figure out.

Enlargement Example

I wanted to see if Robin's math worked in reverse. Does it work to increase a block's size? Let's see.

❋ I want a 12" block but have an 8" pattern.

❋ I start with what I want (12) and divide it by what I've got (8) to get the "proportion number." So, 12 ÷ 8 = 1.5

❋ I move the decimal 2 places to the right, which gives me 150. The pattern needs to be enlarged 150%

❋ If I multiply the original height (8) by the proportion number (1.5), I get 12, the desired block size.

Yes, it works. Robin gives lots more information, but as far as I'm concerned, she won my heart with only this much. Love it. "Ya start with whatcha want, and ya divide it by whatcha got" is now in my math-allergic mind.

A COLORING BOOK GALLERY: THE 14 DESIGNS

ere are the fourteen blocks. How often do we as adults get a chance to color with abandon? Here's your chance to see what the blocks might look like without having to audition and audition, and yes, audition fabrics for each little spot in the block.

By photocopying these pages, you may color 'til your heart is content, making changes with your colored pencils. Then take that colored paper to your fabric stash to get a head start on your fabric mock-up. If nothing else, you will see many things that you do NOT like without wasting fabrics.

Clamshell Block See pages 10 and 14.
ENLARGE 400% for a 12" block.

Feathers I Block See page 63.
ENLARGE 400% for a 12" block.

Feathers II Block See page 19.
ENLARGE 400% for a 12" block.

Fleur de Lis Block See page 23.
ENLARGE 400% for a 12" block.

Harp Block See page 28.
ENLARGE 400% for a 12" block.

Jester Block See page 33.
ENLARGE 400% for a 12" block.

Lindy Loop Block See page 38.
ENLARGE 400% for a 12" block.

Low Vase Block See page 41.
ENLARGE 400% for a 12" block.

Marbles Block See page 47.
ENLARGE 400% for a 12" block.

Philodendron Block See page 53.
ENLARGE 400% for a 12" block.

Piña Block See pages 58 and 64.
ENLARGE 400% for a 12" block.

Sunflower Block See pages 67 and 72.
ENLARGE 400% for a 12" block.

Triad Block See page 74.
ENLARGE 400% for a 12" block.

Tulip Block See page 79.
ENLARGE 400% for a 12" block.

MEET DIANNE S. HIRE

Dianne pushes boundaries! She inspires students to go beyond themselves to a place where they've never been before. They are no longer restricted to a limited palette of design ideas. That's her way of thinking and always has been.

Her husband, cohort in design and love of her life, Terry, has influenced her in many ways... his absurd and beautiful photography inspires Dianne and makes her smile more times than he could ever know.

PHOTO: Terry Hire

Imagine the life of two artists—one playing off the other and the other replaying a similar image, but in another medium. It's an exchange that only can be understood if you are there with them.

About her jump to appliqué—it was something she really didn't know much about when she began. She states, "My goal is to inspire creativity in much the same way as I've done for straight and curved piecing. The wonderful task of taking a traditional quilt-making element to a slightly new design place, bending toward a whole set of what ifs and to allow minds to wander until..., until..., uh, '_____'. That would be you speaking now. You fill in the blank."

Dianne diligently quilting.
Hill-man is missing.
PHOTO: Terry Hire

Enjoy the book

MORE AQS BOOKS

This is only a small selection of the books available from the American Quilter's Society. AQS books are known worldwide for timely topics, clear writing, beautiful color photos, and accurate illustrations and patterns. The following books are available from your local bookseller, quilt shop, or public library.

#8241

#1423

#6295

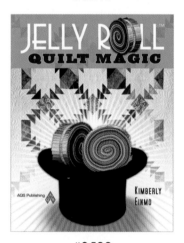

#8523

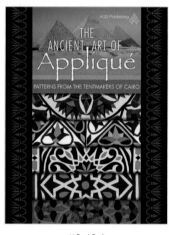

#1416

#8664

#8665

#8532

#8529